LISA:

FOR THE
MEMORIES...

2022

FIRESIDE
REFLECTIONS

. . . a journey through life

brian zimmerman

Fireside Publications LLC
PO Box 11078
Charlotte, North Carolina 28220
www.firesidepublications.com

Printed by Jostens
Charlotte, North Carolina

ISBN# 0-9773047-0-1

jacket and book design by Brian Zimmerman

CONTENTS

I dedicate this book to my parents, Don and Virginia, through whose love and support, my dream has come to fruition . . . and to my daughters, Carie and Julie, as a father's advice to his children.

I give special thanks to my friends, Mary, Leon, Betsey, Claire, Clayton, Donne, Elaine and Calvin who have given of their time and talents to "fine tune" this work.

And to Sherry and Rita, you're the best. Thank you for a special journey.

PREFACE

Poetry comes to us in many forms.

Poetry is emotion felt,
the touch of a child's hand,
a bird's song heard.

Poetry is in the written word,
the taste of a fine wine,
the scent of honeysuckle on an
evening's breeze.

Poetry is marveling at the beauty
of nature.

Poetry speaks differently to us all.

May the pages within speak to each
of you through your heart.   clematis

My head, my heart,
my eyes and my hand
have been guided by
Him through this
work . . . and for that,
I give thanks.

seasons

A crisp winter evening . . .
the air laced with the scent
of a fireplace . . . the sound the
snow makes under foot . . . the
stillness of the gently falling
snow, seeming to take forever
to reach its destination . . .
children singing inside their
warm and cozy abodes . . . the
soft yellow light spilling
from the windows . . . all
unified by the overwhelming
stillness and serenity.

I go there often . . . in my
mind's memories . . . to a
crisp winter evening.

mountain sunset

Life is like the
seasons. We are
born unto the
spring. We grow
and flourish in
the summer. Fall
brings maturity
and poise. Winter
is preparation for
rebirth. It is a
time for resting
and reflecting . . .
and for eternal
peace.

sugar maple

I saw a daffodil today.
Spring, at long last,
has arrived.

I am nourished and
renewed by the coming
of this season more
than any other.

How precious it is
to be alive.

daffodil

Leaves so tender and delicate
at birth . . . so fresh with their
light green color . . . and then
so calming to the eyes and
soul through summer.

Their rustling sounds in autumn
coupled with their palette of
myriad colors, tells us gently
of a peaceful time to come . . . a
time for resting and reflecting.

Like the smell of a fireplace on
a crisp winter's eve, the smell
of burning leaves in autumn stirs
my memories, delights my nostrils,
and quietly prepares me for what's
to come.

Leaves tell us much . . . if we but
listen.   ginkgo

friends

A friendship doesn't just
happen. We must work
at it. It's a partnership
in life.

Close, true, meaningful
friendship is a form of
love that I shall always
cherish. It is a marriage
of the minds, the heart
and the soul . . . a oneness
that is endless. To give
freely of one's self is
to express love.

To experience good things
with close friends is to
be reborn unto the sea
of life.

clematis

Sitting here alone in the
early morning mist, observing
a pair of ducks working their
way along the shoreline, I am
reminded of how fragile life's
relationships can be. Their
preservation is worth every
effort we expend.

And yet, we too often take
their stability for granted.

mallards

Gardening with a friend,
smelling the dampness of
the earth, getting dirt
under your fingernails,
laughing, sharing . . .
these are memories that
will serve me for a
lifetime.

oleander

As I watch my dog
dreaming, listening
to her muffled yelps
as she chases the
squirrels or guards
our home, I find it
difficult to imagine
my life before her.
What a companion
she is . . . such a
simple life.

Oh, that we should
strive to pattern
our lives after
our dogs.

azalea

Live your dreams as you
float down stream on
the river of life.

You are the captain . . .
gather your crew with
care. Your combined
actions will become
the gold that fills
your treasure chest
of memories.

japanese maple

love

Through the dogs I have
befriended in my life,
I have been taught the
true meaning of
unconditional love.
In their hearts is only
love . . . a boundless love.

In the grand scheme
of things . . . I wonder . . .
did He really intend
them to be His little
disciples?

I thank Him for His
four legged teachers.

gloriosa lily

What is it about soft,
soothing music that
reaches down deep
and touches the very
essence of our being?

It whispers in our ear,
touches our heart,
nourishes our soul,
and embraces our
memories.

Music is such an
endearing friend and
companion. Our lives
would not be as rich
without it.

white oak

Love is a gift that can be given only when it is truly understood and felt by the giver.

We must first appreciate and love ourselves before we can offer the gift.

pink dogwood

The phrases "Thank you" and
"I love you" are perhaps the
two most significant phrases
in existence.

Why is it that we choose to
use them so sparingly?

clematis

When we look, do we really
see? By looking within our
hearts, we discover the
rainbow we've been chasing.

When we listen, do we really
hear? Take some quiet time
in nature . . . listen to your
heart.

When we feel an emotion, do
we really perceive? Search
within your heart, the truth
is there.

Let love fill our hearts
with warmth.

honeysuckle

I look forward to meeting you
again someday. Your kind and
gentle approach to life, your
free expressions of love.
These are traits many people
do not have. You were truly
sent by God as His messenger.

You have taught me much
about life. The one thing I will
remember most about you, the
one word that describes you
best . . . is LOVE.

I look forward to spending
time with you again someday.

double hibiscus

From the tree
comes the seed.
And through the
seed the tree
lives on.

Through loving
and sharing, the
tree is eternal.

deodara cedar (immature cone)

Why is it that we feel so
close to someone at their
passing?

At that point in their life's
journey, our emotions matter
not. How much better it would
have been had we expressed our
feelings during their walk on
earth.

Our lives are today. Let us
express our feelings for each
other...today . . . before it's
too late.

sweet peas and blackeyed susan

The true essence of being human, surfaces during a funeral . . . giving us a brief glimpse of the human spirit.

We witness love as if it were a three dimensional entity. We can really "see" what love is. We can touch it, smell it, taste it in our tears. We can hear its boundless resound in the beating of our own heart.

At a funeral, we begin to think of our own mortality. We realize that we too will be the focus of attention one day . . . at a gathering of our friends and relatives . . . to pay homage to our life . . . our spirit . . . the essence of our being.

crab apple

A friend shared this with
me shortly after she lost
her husband to cancer.

Just before his death, he
asked her "When I die, will
you write me a letter?"
Her response was "Where
shall I send it?" "Don't
bother," he replied, "I'll
read over your shoulder as
you write."

The love they shared was
truly beautiful . . . and I thank
her for sharing this story.

It is beauty like this that
we all must experience more
of. This is God's love . . .
and it will sustain us.

chinese clematis

family

Yesterday, the gentle spring
breezes brought to my nose
the scent of lavender, the
fragrance my grandmother
wore. She's fifteen years
since gone, but the scent
triggered my memory of her.
It was so real. I felt so
close to her at that moment,
as if I could reach out to
receive her gentle touch.

I wish I could.

fringe tree

A wise man once told me "It takes a better person to say no when he knows he is right, than to say yes and comply with the wishes of the majority." This advice has served me well through the years.

Thanks Dad.

red maple

Mother's breast gives
you food to begin your
journey. But, mother's
love will nourish you
for a lifetime.

saucer magnolia

She came to us that
May day, with her hair
of gold. She entered
our lives like a yellow
butterfly. Now that she
has moved on, we sense
her presence at the sight
of every yellow swallowtail.

bull thistle

Loving one's children
doesn't necessarily mean
that we always have to
like them . . . but we will
always love them . . .
no matter what.

flowering cherry

With baby on my back
and a thermos of hot tea
sweetened with honey, we
struck out on that snowy
day in search of sassafras.

I rested her against a tree
stump while I began to pull
up sassafras roots from the
yet unfrozen earth. When
the root broke unexpectedly,
I fell on my backside. My
young companion found the
scene to be quite humorous
and proceeded to fill the
forest with her tiny
laughter.

It seems like yesterday.

sassafras

We danced to music not
heard, my daughter and I.
She, employing skills I
had taught her as a little
girl, stealthily stalking
the illusive swan. We
moved in harmony, not a
word spoken nor a signal
given, each moving to push
the swan into position for
that photographic moment
when magic happens.

We danced to music not
heard, my daughter and I.

swan

Courage is facing each new day
with a sense of curiosity, looking
through benevolent eyes gilded by
age, humility and tenacity, but
salted with a portion of humor.

Courage is being able to bid
the hand that life has dealt, by
surveying it through the eyes of
youth, looking past the limits
it has imposed, finding a way to
feign and finesse, ever striving
to fulfill the contract . . . yet, ever
knowing that if faced with certain
failure, you'll get up and try again.

Courage is the example my parents
have set for me to emulate. I pray
that I can at least match their
example for my progeny.

blackeyed susan

nature

To watch a hawk soar, endlessly,
without apparent effort, fills
me with awe.

To experience the rarity of a
rainbow, makes my heart as full
as the sky.

The clouds, they float so gently,
their wisps . . . their swirls . . . in a
sky so blue.

It's the simple things in life
that possess rare beauty . . . if
we but stop and observe.

clouds

I feel a closeness to the
sea . . . like a surrogate
mother . . . as if I might
have been born of her
womb.

She nutures me. She is
timeless. She is endless
fascination . . . like life
itself . . . tranquil, yet
violent.

I do so love the sea.

ocean sunrise

In my youth, I thought
I had witnessed some
spectacular fall color . . .
but then, I had never been
to the mountains.

I recall that first fall
visit to the mountains.
The colors were so vivid
and vibrant . . . as if, with
His own hand, God had
painted each tree from
a palette of love.

sugar maple

I feel comfortable
in the forest. Nature
is a true friend. We
understand each other.
We are as one . . . nature
and I.

Nature tells everything
in her own language . . .
patience. For one who
goes through life in
a hurry, for one who
refuses to take the
time to listen, her
voice is inaudible.

forest silhouette

How do we explain to a sightless
person the wonders and beauty
of nature? Are we not all a little
blind to some of these things?
Our sight is only improved
through the knowledge and
awareness that some of these
things do indeed exist. The
beauty is in the educated eye,
if and only if, we know what it
is we are seeing. To see, we
must first observe. To know
what we are seeing is to add
another dimension to our senses.

To look beyond what the eye
can see is to discover. Discovery
is food for the imagination.
Without discovery and
imagination, the mind is no
longer fertile. Let us explore
beyond . . . let us live.

lacecap hydrangea

life

For those of us who
have the courage to
see ourselves, and
then the strength
to love ourselves
in spite of what
we have seen, the
Creator will reward
us with a sense of
fulfillment and
peace.

azalea

When we feel abandoned,
look to His spirit within . . .
the essence of life . . . for
there shall our needs
be met.

dogwood

Life is so full of joy, if we
but learn to relax and take
the time to appreciate and
experience it. Let us slow our
hurried pace and experience
the true joy of life . . . for
today is not the first day
of the rest of our lives . . .
our life is today.

wisteria

Waiting is such a difficult
task. It's as if time were
standing still . . . or moving
backwards.

How can time be so precious,
yet we wish it away as if it
were a worthless commodity?
It's a sin to waste time . . .
we are given so little of it.

Time is one of the few things
in today's world that we have
complete control over . . .
or do we?

I wonder.

tulips

Our limited time on earth
is compressed between
yesterday and tomorrow.
God has given us that
precious gift of life
for just one day.

Tomorrow is man's way of
marking time. There are
no guarantees that we
will have another day . . .
there is only hope.

Yesterday is a memory.
May we be nourished by
its beauty.

Today, we should rejoice
and live a lifetime.

Enjoy God's gift and
use it wisely.

sugar maple

To become successful
at what we choose to
do for our life's work,
a price must first be
paid. If we are willing
to pay that price, and
if we truly love what
we do, it is then that
we discover one of
life's true joys.

magnolia

Always honor
the voice of
your inner
child.

ducklings

ethics

Wear yourself on the outside. The way you look, the way you feel, the manner in which you present yourself . . . that's the real you.

lacecap hydrangea

Sometimes, no matter how hard
we try, our feelings cannot be
expressed in words. The words
do not exist. It is only when
we are in tune with each other
that we can hear what is being
said.

It is not the words we speak
that portray the true meaning
of what we feel. We speak also
through our eyes, through body
movements, and above all, from
the heart. We may say one
thing, but through our image,
be portraying something
totally different. We must
feel what we say in order to
truly convey our meaning.

ocean sunset

It is said that the
pen is mightier
than the sword.

Both the pen and the
tongue can produce
a wound much deeper
and more lasting
than any sword.

Yet skillfully and
lovingly used, words
are as a surgeon's
scalpel cutting away
the proud flesh of
many years.

Let us be mindful of
the words we choose
and the manner in
which they are used.

chaste tree

Hatred is likened to a cancer
that ravages our hearts, turning
them cold and ugly. Nothing life
has to offer is worth the price
of hatred.

Fear spawns hatred. Once we
conquer fear, there's no reason
to hate.

Ignorance leads us to hate.
Once we learn, hatred is
meaningless.

Hatred is pointless . . . it serves
no purpose. It's a waste of our
time, energy and emotions.

May warmth and beauty spill from
our hearts to wash away the seeds
of hate. May our days together
be spent in harmony.

pink dogwood

wisdom

Living is likened to a journey
on the sea of life. As you
float along on peaceful
waters, you may, without
warning, encounter an
approaching flood. Navigating
these turbulent waters is
sometimes a better choice
than attempting to alter the
course of the flood.

Tenacity and His endearing
support, will keep you afloat.
The buoyancy created will
afford you the opportunity
to extract a tiny pearl of
wisdom that will assist
you in weathering your
next flood.

duckings

Be not afraid to try again
after having failed at one
or numerous attempts.

Keep steadfast your vision
of accomplishment . . . not
your failed attempts.

The body gives birth to
the seeds we nourish.
We need add only a
little courage to
bring forth new life.

savannah holly

Seek not to know all
things . . . some must
be accepted on blind
faith.

Go not outside yourself
to find inner peace, for
what you seek resides
within.

Become quiet and listen
to His inner voice for
guidance . . . from within,
true wisdom will emerge.

petunias

We have been entrusted
with but one life . . . to
do with as we see fit.

Let us make the right
decisions throughout
the course of our
lives. Let us give
our all.

Let our existence have
substance and purpose . . .
for we have been entrusted
with but one life to live.

swan

The mighty oak, with its
stalwart dignity, reminds
us to remain steadfast in
our mission, to listen not
to the council of fools,
but to be ever mindful
of the wisdom in our
own heart.

black oak

reflections

Listen to the music of
the wind through a pine
forest, or the soothing
sounds of a mountain
stream. It's a rhapsody
of peace and tranquility.

bloodroot

A gentle summer rain
falling on your face . . .
like a kiss from the
Creator. How beautiful
His kiss makes the garden
look...with droplets of
rain still clinging to
the leaves.

How clean the air
smells. Everything is
so fresh . . . almost as if
it were spring again.

Imagine it . . . being
able to experience
spring so many
times.

clematis

What we need in our lives
is a little less clutter . . .
and a lot more simplicity.

tulips

The music a fire plays,
the scents that fill our
nostrils, the mystique
of the figures dancing
upon the logs, the
romance of a fireplace . . .
ah, there is nothing like it.

buckeye

When I contemplate
the meaning of life, I am
reminded of many things:
the way a child's hand
feels in mine; the soft
voice of assurance from
one you love; a tender
kiss from the lips of
your grandmother; a
firm and lingering hug
when you needed it most,
words of praise when
deserved, kind words of
council upon request . . .
and then there's His
touch . . . to let you
know you are not
alone.

mountain waterfall

It's so quiet between the
succession of endless waves.
You can almost hear the sun
slicing through the morning
air . . . the air so crisp with
the fresh scent of the sea.

Watching the killdeer race
across the moist sand in
search of food . . . the
occasional sound of a gull . . .
the thrill at the sight of
porpoise breaking the surface .
To share, with someone you love,
a scene so beautiful as a
sunrise, is to experience what
heaven must be like.

ocean sunrise

Thank you, everyone, for
sharing my musings. I
hope I have given you
reason to perceive the
world with heightened
senses.

With a light heart,
may your continued
journey through life
be filled with peace.

A GIFT OF MEMORIES

FOR . . .
- staff
- clients
- family
- friends
- yourself

FOR CELEBRATING . . .
- holidays
- birthdays
- anniversaries
- weddings

FOR SAYING . . .
- thank you
- I love you
- I miss you
- you make me smile

SAVE FOR . . .
- that special occasion

FIRESIDE PUBLICATIONS
www.firesidepublications.com